Iowa

IOWA

A Buddy Book
by

Julie Murray

ABDO
Publishing Company

VISIT US AT
www.abdopub.com

Published by ABDO Publishing Company, 4940 Viking Drive, Edina, Minnesota 55435.

Printed in the United States.

Edited by: Sarah Tieck
Contributing Editor: Michael P. Goecke
Graphic Design: Deb Coldiron, Maria Hosley
Image Research: Sarah Tieck
Photographs: Brand X Pictures, Clipart.com, Corbis, Effigy Mounds National Monument (National Park Service), EyeWire, Getty Images, One Mile Up, PhotoDisc. Special thanks to the National Scenic Byways Program (www.byways.org) for use of the photo on page 21.

Library of Congress Cataloging-in-Publication Data

Murray, Julie, 1969-
   Iowa / Julie Murray.
      p. cm. — (The United States)
   Includes bibliographical references and index.
   ISBN 1-59197-674-X
      1. Iowa—Juvenile literature. I. Title.

F621.3.M87 2005
977.7—dc22

                                        2004062723

Table Of Contents

A Snapshot Of Iowa 4

Where Is Iowa? 8

Fun Facts 14

Cities And The Capital 16

Famous Citizens 18

Loess Soil 20

Effigy Mounds National Monument 22

The Amish 25

A History Of Iowa 28

A State Map 30

Important Words 31

Web Sites 31

Index .32

A Snapshot Of Iowa

When people think of Iowa they think of farms. The state is home to almost 100,000 farms. Iowa has dark, rich, fertile soil that is ideal for growing crops.

Iowa's landscape is covered with farms.

Corn is an important crop in Iowa.

Iowa is the leading producer of corn in the United States. Iowa is also known for its dairy, cattle, and hog farming. Iowa is located in the middle of the United States. This part of the country is sometimes called "the heartland of America."

Iowa has many dairy and cattle farms like this one.

There are 50 states in the United States. Every state is different. Every state has an official state nickname. Iowa is sometimes called the "Hawkeye State." Iowa's nickname honors the leader of the Sauk Native American tribe. His name was chief Black Hawk. The Sauk Native Americans lived in Iowa in the 1800s.

Iowa became the 29th state on December 28, 1846. It has 56,276 square miles (145,754 sq km). It is the 25th-largest state. It is home to 2,926,324 people.

Many people in Iowa live in small towns.

Where Is Iowa?

There are four parts of the United States. Each part is called a region. Each region is in a different area of the country. The United States Census Bureau says the four regions are the Northeast, the South, the Midwest, and the West.

Four Regions of the United States of America

ALASKA

WASHINGTON

MONTANA

NORTH DAKOTA

VERMONT

MAINE

OREGON

IDAHO

MINNESOTA

WISCONSIN

NEW
HAMPSHIRE

MASSACHUSETTS

SOUTH DAKOTA

MICHIGAN

NEW
YORK

RHODE ISLAND
CONNECTICUT

WYOMING

PENNSYLVANIA

NEVADA

UTAH

IOWA

NEW JERSEY

NEBRASKA

ILLINOIS

INDIANA

OHIO

DELAWARE

Washington D.C.

CALIFORNIA

COLORADO

KANSAS

MISSOURI

WEST
VIRGINIA

VIRGINIA

MARYLAND

KENTUCKY

ARIZONA

NEW MEXICO

OKLAHOMA

ARKANSAS

TENNESSEE

NORTH CAROLINA

SOUTH
CAROLINA

MISSISSIPPI

ALABAMA

GEORGIA

TEXAS

LOUISIANA

FLORIDA

HAWAII

West	Midwest	South	Northeast

People sled on snowy winter days in Iowa.

Iowa is located in the Midwest region of the United States. People living in Iowa experience all types of weather. Iowa has four seasons. These seasons are spring, summer, fall, and winter. It is cool in spring and fall, and cold and snowy during winter.

During the summer it is hot and humid. This is perfect weather for growing crops.

Hot, humid summer weather can also cause tornadoes. Iowa has more than 30 tornadoes every year.

Iowa is part of "Tornado Alley."

The state of Iowa is bordered by six other states. Minnesota lies to the north. Wisconsin and Illinois are to the east. Missouri is to the south of Iowa. Nebraska and South Dakota lie to the west. Rivers create Iowa's east and west borders. The Mississippi River forms the eastern border. The Missouri River forms the western border of the state.

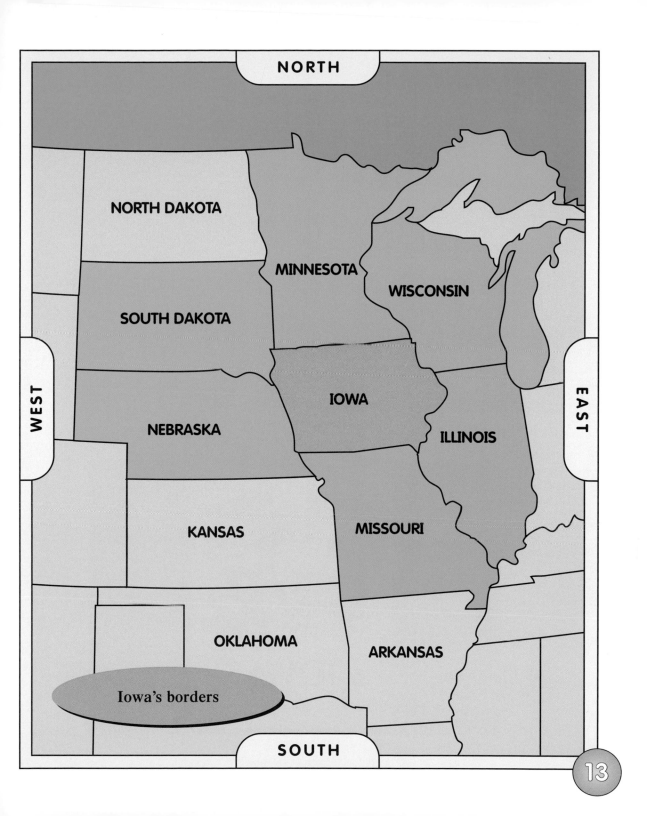

NORTH

NORTH DAKOTA

MINNESOTA

WISCONSIN

SOUTH DAKOTA

WEST

IOWA

EAST

NEBRASKA

ILLINOIS

KANSAS

MISSOURI

OKLAHOMA

ARKANSAS

Iowa's borders

SOUTH

13

Iowa

State abbreviation: IA

State nickname: The Hawkeye State

State capital: Des Moines

State motto: Our Liberties We Prize and Our Rights We Will Maintain

Statehood: December 28, 1846, 29th state

Population: 2,926,324, ranks 30th

Land area: 56,276 square miles (145,754 sq km), ranks 25th

State flag: Adopted in 1921

State song: "The Song of Iowa"

State government: Three branches: legislative, executive, and judicial

Average July temperature: 75°F (24°C)

Average January temperature: 19°F (-7°C)

State flower:
Wild rose

State bird:
Eastern goldfinch

State tree:
Oak

Cities And The Capital

Des Moines is Iowa's largest city. It is also the capital city of the state. Des Moines is located in the south central part of the state. The city lies along the Des Moines River. Des Moines is home to the Iowa State Fair. Many insurance companies are located there. So is Meredith Corporation, which publishes magazines all over the country.

The skyline of Des Moines.

The second-largest city in Iowa is Cedar Rapids. This industrial city is located in east central Iowa.

Davenport is Iowa's third-largest city. It lies along the Mississippi River. It is in the southeastern part of the state. It is one of four cities called the Quad Cities.

Famous Citizens

Herbert Hoover (1874-1964)

Herbert Hoover was one of the famous people who have called Iowa home. Herbert Hoover was president of the United States from 1929 to 1933. He was the 31st president of the United States. He was born in West Branch. He was the president when the stock market  crashed in 1929. This led to the Great Depression. This was a time when many people were very poor. The entire country struggled.

Herbert Hoover

Famous Citizens

John Wayne (1907-1979)

John Wayne was born in Winterset in 1907. He was a famous actor. Many people remember him for playing cowboys. His first classic Western was *Stagecoach*. He appeared in more than 150 movies. He won an Academy Award for *True Grit* in 1969.

John Wayne

Loess Soil

Loess is a special kind of soil. Sioux City is known for its loess bluffs. There are loess hills throughout western Iowa.

Loess is usually a yellow color. It is tiny mineral pieces. Loess is carried by the wind. When it lands on the ground, it becomes topsoil. The loess soil is very fertile.

The loess soil makes formations like bluffs and hills.

Effigy Mounds
National Monument

More than 2,000 years ago, Native Americans were the only people who lived in Iowa. These early people were called the Eastern Woodland Native Americans.

The Eastern Woodland Native Americans were known for making special piles of dirt. These are called Effigy Mounds. The mounds are made in many different shapes.

Many of the mounds are built to look like animals, such as bears.

Today, people can still see the mounds. They are at Effigy Mound National Monument. This monument was created in 1949. People can see more than 195 preserved mounds. Some of the mounds are 300 feet (91 m) long.

The Amish

Iowa is one of five states in the United States with a large community of Amish people. Amish people live on farms.

The Amish people grow their own food on farms.

The Amish are a group of people who believe in living a simple life free of modern things. This means they do not have cars or televisions. They use horses and buggies for transportation and grow almost all of the food they eat on their farms. The men and women dress in plain clothes that are sewn by the women.

The Amish people don't have cars. They ride in buggies pulled by horses.

The Amish are known for their great woodworking. People can buy Amish-made furniture in many places around the United States.

Iowa

1673: A Frenchman and a French-Canadian man explore the Mississippi River. They discover Iowa. They are Father Jacques Marquette and Louis Jolliet.

1788: French-Canadian Julien Dubuque is Iowa's first settler.

1803: President Thomas Jefferson arranges for the United States to buy Iowa as part of the Louisiana Purchase.

1804: Meriwether Lewis and William Clark explore Iowa. Sergeant Charles Floyd, a member of their group, dies in Sioux City on August 20. He is the first and only member of the expedition to die.

1846: Iowa becomes the 29th state on December 28.

1867: The first railroad goes across Iowa.

1895: Stark Brothers Nursery starts growing the Red Delicious apple.

1913: The Keokuk Dam on the Mississippi River is finished.

The capitol building in Des Moines.

1946: Iowa celebrates its centennial.

1993: The Mississippi, Missouri, and Des Moines rivers flood. This causes $2 billion in damages.

2005: Famous talk-show host Johnny Carson, a native of Corning, dies.

Cities in Iowa

Dubuque

Sioux City

Cedar Rapids

West Branch

Davenport

Des Moines ⭐

Winterset

Corning

Important Words

capital a city where government leaders meet.

centennial 100-year anniversary.

humid air that is damp or moist.

Louisiana Purchase a deal where the United States bought land from France. Part of this land later became Iowa.

modern the way of life in the present time.

nickname a name that describes something special about a person or a place.

tornado a storm cloud that is shaped like a funnel and swirls fast, destroying homes and cities.

Web Sites

To learn more about Iowa, visit ABDO Publishing Company on the World Wide Web. Web site links about Iowa are featured on our Book Links page. These links are routinely monitored and updated to provide the most current information available.

www.abdopub.com

Index

Amish	**25, 26, 27**
Black Hawk	**6**
Cedar Rapids	**17**
Clark, William	**28**
corn	**5**
Davenport	**17**
Des Moines	**14, 16, 17, 29**
Des Moines River	**16, 29**
Dubuque, Julien	**28**
Effigy Mounds National Monument	**22, 23, 24**
farms	**4, 5, 6, 25, 26**
Floyd, Charles	**28**
Great Depression	**18**
Hoover, Herbert	**18**
Illinois	**12**
Jefferson, Thomas	**28**
Jolliet, Louis	**28**
Lewis, Meriwether	**28**
loess	**20, 21**
Marquette, Jacques	**28**
Midwest	**8, 9, 10**
Minnesota	**12**
Mississippi River	**12, 17, 28, 29**
Missouri	**12**
Missouri River	**12, 29**
Native Americans	**6, 22, 23**
Nebraska	**12**
Northeast	**8, 9**
Sioux City	**20, 28**
South	**8, 9**
South Dakota	**12**
tornado	**11**
United States Census Bureau	**8**
Wayne, John	**19**
weather	**10, 11, 15**
West	**8, 9**
West Branch	**18**
Winterset	**19**
Wisconsin	**12**